THO

THOUGHTS

A collection of short poems

Written By

Keith Hearn

ISBN-13:978-1985693534
ISBN – 10-1985693526

THOUGHTS

Acknowledgements

The past year has been the most
challenging of times for me

On the other hand, I have found many
strengths I never knew I possessed

Writing poetry makes me feel so calm
and at peace

I hope the reader will find at least one
poem which may resonate with the
reader

Relax and imagine you are with me
when you are reading the poems
within the book

ENJOY WHATEVER BRINGS
YOU HAPPINESS IN LIFE

LIFE IS FAR TOO SHORT

THOUGHTS

TUNNEL

When will it ever end? It is just like a never ending dark and dank tunnel

Being inside the never ending tunnel there does not seem to be a light at the or an ending

Life sometimes is just like a tread mill standing still and just running on the spot

Always thinking when will the good times ever come back

Suddenly, the tunnel ends, and the daylight suddenly floods the carriages

THOUGHTS

Somewhat like life itself suddenly light breaks through the darkness and once again life feels so good

COLOURS

The very first signs of spring are in the
air and spring can be seen in all its
glory

After so many months of darkness
with just blacks and greys filling the
sky

The whites of the snowdrops are first
to appear followed by the bright yellow
flowers of daffodils, colour is on its
way

Spring is on its way and the spring
light lasts so much longer during the
hours of daytime

THOUGHTS

The short dark days of winter are once again banished for another season

THOUGHTS

TRUE LOVE

True love comes without any conditions

TOUCH

To feel the softness of another's skin is
so electrifying

The feel sends electricity coursing
through my body

Touch is such a normal and everyday
thing and is taken for granted

Touch can make two people feel they
are wanted by someone else and
nothing need be said

But when someone is alone it is all that
is needed

LOVE

Love is such a powerful word

*At times it can be used in such a
throw away manner*

*The word love can mean so many
different things to so many people*

TRUST

Only trust oneself in life

As it is only you who will let yourself down

And it is only you who is to blame

GIVE UP

Many people will give up on finding
love

They turn to living just for their work

When suddenly, love smacks them
between the eyes

Work then takes second place

STRAIGHT AND NARROW

When will life's woes cease

Just when life seems on the straight
and narrow

Something comes along and knocks one
off the track

Its seems far away to get oneself back
on the straight and narrow

ORGANISED CHAOS

Organised chaos all around and so
many people sat eating and drinking

People ordering food and drink

The pub staff escorting people to their
table taking the many orders for food

It is obvious the pub is jammed pack

In the end everyone is served and are
very happy

Just a thought how can people work in
such organised chaos

THOUGHTS

BE YOURSELF

Just be yourself

Don't let anyone change the perfect you

FIRST LIGHT

The first months of spring brings out
the strong spring sun

The sun breaks through the darkened
skies to warm up the cold ground

The early morning light makes one
thinks they have slept in

Only to find it is still very much early
morning

The mind still hasn't adapted from the
dark winter mornings

NATURE

The first inkling of spring has arrived
to the relief of both nature and man

It feels like a blessing

The spring light helps to wake nature
from its hibernation and its winter
slumber

There is so much energy within the
land

Wildlife begins to wake from its
slumber and from the deep winters
sleep

LIPS

The woman with the bright red lips

How polite she was talking to a total stranger

So well spoken, and very well mannered

Someone with an engaging smile

But there is no getting away from the draw of those bright red lips

IGNORED

When you know someone just does not
care

When she sees you and you realise
there is nothing there

She ignores you and shows no interest
what so ever

It is time to move on and leave her
alone

That is her problem and not yours

SOMEONE FOR EVERYONE

We Are not placed on this world to be alone

The world is such a large place

Somewhere there is someone for everyone

Never give up because remember there is someone out there feeling just as you do

VULNERABILITY

To attack someone who is vulnerable
and feeling raw

To do so is so base and just shows how
horrible and just shows how horrible
that person really is

Vulnerability in another seems to
attract the worse within others

Is it a sign of weakens in the one who is
carrying out the attacking?

We all become vulnerable at some time
in life

And as such should know better

THOUGHTS

STILL AIR

The air all around is so still the snow is
covering the land

Each sound is amplified in the stillness

The crack of a branch having been
stood on resonates in the air

The bird's song lingers a little longer
within the frozen wood

Foot steps when hitting the snow make
a crunching noise

The intense whiteness of the snow
makes the darkest of most things stand
out against the whiteness of the snow

22

FIRST LIGHT

*The first months of the spring sun,
breaks through the dark sky*

*The sun makes such a pleasant change
from those far off dark wintery
evenings*

*The earth is waking up from its winter
slumber*

*The first shoots of spring appear in the
soil, it is such a pleasant sight*

*The yellow flowers of the daffodils are
appearing all around*

*It is the first signs of the sunnier and
warmer days are finally on the way*

FENCE PANELS

In the quaint English village where everything seems at first sight just right?

With its nice houses and well-kept gardens

A wiggly wonky fence appears

Just to throw the quaint picture village out of sorts

It is the only irregular thing in the village

It helps keep people on their toes and gives the villages something to talk about

DREAMS

As soon as I saw her I could not keep
my eyes from her

It was so awful of me to just stand
staring in her direction, but I just
could not help myself

I do not know what it was, for me
there was a magnetism towards her

She told me she hadn't previously
noticed me staring at her?

One can only dream for someone so
pretty and very pleasant as her to
come into my life

THOUGHTS

Dreams are so very personal and belong to no one else they are yours alone, to be shared with someone special

It is of our choosing if we share our dreams with another

Other people are only allowed to hear of another person's dreams when it feels just right or if the dream has come true

Dreams are so personal

IGNORE

When you know someone is not
interested in you it is such a horrible
feeling cuts to the quick

When she notices you and there is
nothing forthcoming, it is then that
you realise there is nothing there

She ignores you and shows no interest
or emotion

It is time to move on and forget that
person and move on

Never look back

FLIGHTY

Life is so strange, there she was sitting
in the same pub

She knows full well how attractive she
is

But she isn't the person for me

If we were an item could I ever trust
her?

I know deep down I could never trust
her

She is far too flighty for me

THOUGHTS

OH WHY

I thought I had made such an
impression on you

Only to find I hadn't made any
impression at all

We live separate lives

You don't acknowledge me

So very sad

SOMETIMES

Sometimes we all make mistakes

You are so interesting but real life is so different

She knew all along she did not like me, but never said

But over time you began to make it so obvious

Your dislike of me made me feel so cold

STRUCTURE

Such wonderful bone structure makes
her even more prettier

She looks so pretty and loves her
pictures

She is free spirit

Her tattoos tell a story possibly her
very own story

She is one hell of an artist

Her paintings have so much feeling in
them

A WINTERS DAY

It is a typical British pub on a winters
day

Snow is laying on the ground and
drifting across the fields

There it is in the distant standing so
proud in the snow it is the local pub

Its lights glowing against the darkened
skies

Inside is an inviting log fire pushing
out the heat around the pub

Inside it is so comforting and inviting
no one wants to leave

QUESTIONS WITH OUT ANSWERS

So why did you ever want to contact
me in the first place?

To then never want to meet with me?

So many questions are left unanswered

Was I so naïve to have not realised you
would have never agree to meet me

I suppose as an elderly man it was just
a dream?

But I have to say my life has been so
enriched by you

THOUGHTS

And now I feel so empty and lost

*For you, life carries on and it may
have just been a game to you?*

*Who knows only you know the true
answer to the question*

SHARING

I don't have much, but what I do have
could have been shared with you

All I ever wanted to be was someone
who cared for you

To others it may have seemed like
being needy and wanting who knows
what it was I felt for you

There are so many people who would
never understand how I felt for you

My love for you was free and without
conditions

LIFE

Life is made up of so many tiers and levels

If life was smooth and easy, then it would be so very boring and predictable

Life isn't like a book

If it was it would be so easy

Life's journey would be so easy much easier

Life is full of surprises

It certainly keeps me on my toes

THOUGHTS

HOW WELL HAVE WE DONE?

How well have we done in life, what is
the measurement of success?

To come from a city with such
depravation

Having been brought up with a
mother who couldn't read or write

As children the Beano and Dandy
were our teachers and so much fun

The Commando comic helped in our
reading skills

Reading words such as "achtung" and
"spitfeur" taught so much

37

THOUGHTS

It did not mean we read comics, but it helped

Now in the future we are extremely successful in our chosen professions

DREAMER

Is everyone a dreamer?

Being a dreamer comforts one
against the real world

The problem with dreams they
have a habit of bursting

A dreamer never seems to make
a mark on the world

My life has become somewhat
like a dream

Who wants to live in a dream?

THOUGHTS

*The realities of life have a habit
of smacking a dreamer hard
across the face*

*No-one believes in a dreamer
because dreams never come true*

IDEA

You have no idea of how I truly feel about you

You are oblivious to my true feelings towards you

But someone of your age why would you know about how I feel

Your body looks divine

Should I be feeling this way about you?

Who knows because I don't

NORMAL

My world isn't what one could
ever call "normal"

I seem to wait for the
opportunity for my life to move
on

Others may feel I am not living a
"normal" life whatever it is?

My life in my eyes is very
"normal"

Who knows what normal means

Perhaps those who are "normal"
are now in the minority?

MEET

Why could you never meet with
me?

You hurt me to the quick and left
me in such pain

I thought I was a fool perhaps I
was who knows?

You turned my life upside down

All I ever wanted was to meet
for a coffee

What was so wrong with that?

Because of a cup of coffee, we can
never meet one another

As hard as I tried you refused to
meet or made every excuse for
not able to meet such a shame

Now look at us

Alone

SOMEONE

My life is full of loneliness I often
dream of meeting someone to
make me feel whole once more

Is it too much to ask for?

I don't mean just anyone I meant
a loving person to share our lives
together

To then share the ups and downs
of life the upsets, the heartache
and happiness

Is it all too much to ask for?

Surely not

MISTAKES

Did I make a mistake in life who
will ever know the truth?

What have I done it all started in
my twenties and had a profound
effect on me in later life

It is high time to cease thinking
like that

If I carry on it could destroy
everything I have

I cannot carry on thinking this
way

It is time to forget my mistakes
and to begin to live life to the full

THOUGHTS

Guilt is a terrible feeling as it eats away at the soul

QUESTIONS

Who and what are you

You have never opened up to me
is it because you are hiding a
terrible secret from me?

You gloss over my questions

You don't even know my name,
and it makes me feel so angry, at
not knowing my name after so
long

I am very open with you

But on the other hand, you have
told me nothing about yourself

THOUGHTS

Because of the way you have
treated me we will never meet

It is so sad and such a shame

EVIL

There are so many kind people in
the world

There are also terrible people

When we are born we know
nothing of this world or the
hatred

No-one is born evil

Some are fed the drivel by adults
who should know better

The adults begin to fill the child's
mind with such hatred towards
others

THOUGHTS

*We are all human no matter
what skin colour we are born
with*

*We are born with love pounding
in our hearts and not the hatred*

A TIME TO DREAM

Is dreaming a weakness

I dream all the time

I sometimes hope my dreams can
come true

Who knows where my dreams
might take me

Life is a long journey

Who knows what might be
around the corner?

We can only but dream

Who knows?

NAIVITY

Does she realise how she comes
across to others?

She comes across as very naïve
person

Perhaps she isn't as naïve as she
seems to make out or perhaps it
is just a smoke screen?

She is very angelic

I know not what goes through
her mind

My time is not her time in life

My time is coming to an end

LEARN

Do we ever learn from our
mistakes?

Of course, we don't far from it

I have made many mistakes in
my life

I have learnt many lessons from
my mistakes

The big question is have I learnt
anything from my past mistakes?

The obvious answer is a
resounding no!!

LIFE DERAILED

My life is so upside down

I no longer know where I am
heading for

It is foggy and without any
direction

Perhaps you will help me get
back on track

I dream of having a loving
person in my life

I don't seem to have settled I feel
so restless

THOUGHTS

Perhaps you have derailed life's
journey

Yes you

HAPPINESS

Sat beneath a tree in the
beautiful English countryside
sitting in the full glare of the
morning sun

Rolling fields stretching for miles
further than the eye can see

Not another soul in sight it feels
relaxing

Not everyone is so lucky to find a
spot to be able to shut out the
manic world all around

A world seemingly in such chaos

THOUGHTS

People not knowing what will happen next and daring to switch on the news in the morning

To be able to sit in the countryside and to immerse into one's thoughts is indeed such rare luxury to have

FIVE MINUTES

To walk out of the front door of
the house and within minutes to
be able to wander in the
countryside is just so wonderful

As a child the only countryside
were the large municipal parks
surrounding Liverpool

But even so they are the lungs of
the city

I never take for granted the gift
of living in the beautiful
countryside surrounding the
ancient city of Winchester

THOUGHTS

There are not many people who are lucky to have what I have

Lucky is not the word to use, it is one that sums up how I feel about the place I now find myself living in

RUN

*The world is being run by people
on the face of things don't care
for others who aren't as powerful
as they are*

*It was only months earlier these
people were democratically
elected to run their countries*

*They forget that they have been
elected by the people to serve the
people*

*I am afraid what has happened
recently the world has become so
unstable is frightening to see
what they the elected are doing
to their own people*

THOUGHTS

*Is the world on the brink of a
third world war?*

We shall see, only time will tell

*A war which could destroy much
of the planet*

*But when will mother nature
takes her revenge only time will
truly tell*

*Nobody controls or rules mother
nature*

*It is her who controls each one of
us*

SELECTIVE

*Do we give up dreaming as we
get older?*

Or do we dream even more?

*As children dreams are ten a
penny*

*As we grow older dreams are
more selective and targeted and
more meaningful*

*As young people dreams we all
chase our dreams some come true
but many falls by the wayside*

*That is until we are older and
never wish to let a dream go*

THOUGHTS

Dreams do come true no matter how old a person is

And no matter what the dream is

FRUSTRATION

My frustrations simmer beneath
the surface and suddenly the
frustration boils over

No one ever makes me feel so
frustrated as you do

I think do you seem do it
deliberately

Why can't you take what we
have to another level?

What is stopping you

I don't have a clue to why you
are so reluctant to move things
on

THOUGHTS

To the next level

*Who knows what goes on in your
head because I certainly don't*

A PICTURE

*Most mornings you paint a
picture of a beautiful woman*

I cannot see you

*You bar me from meeting with
you*

*Something which is so normal to
most people*

But not for you

*You keep on telling me you are
not ready to meet*

Why

THOUGHTS

What is so wrong in wanting to meet you

Perhaps you have two heads

You tease me so

One morning your pictures will disappear for ever?

WHAT DO YOU WANT FORM ME?

I often wonder what you want
from me

Apart from my brain which isn't
much to like

As I am an aging old man

You are a beautiful young
woman

My thoughts about you are so
mixed up

My lasting thoughts are still
"what do you want from me"?

MOVE ON

My heart tells me that all of this
is good, if only we could be
together

My head tells me there is
something wrong with the whole
setup

You would never look twice at
me if we were to ever in the
street

My head tells me to go with my
gut feeling

And to run a mile in the opposite
direction

ARTIST

Oh, how I look forward to your
social media posts

You are so talented

your posts are very funny and
inspirational

Up all night painting and
producing fine pieces of artwork

How I have laughed at some of
your posts

Deep down there is a serious
message to be portrayed

THOUGHTS

*Keep up your good work, my
lady of mystery*

*I have been so inspired by what
you say and what you do*

IT IS OUT THERE

Things could change for the better only if you want it to happen

All you need to do, is to let me into your world

You push me away at every hurdle

I will not beg you to let me in

It can only happen if only you want it to happen

I cannot force you, if it isn't what you want

THOUGHTS

*You see my time is running out
and it will be the last time I find
happiness in my lifetime*

*All I can say happiness is out
there*

*Only you can let it in and light
up your heart*

THE BAR STOOL

The bar stool sits alone most of
the day

That is until half past five in the
afternoon

It is when the stool comes into its
own

It sits at a prime location within
the bar area on the corner and
close to the beer taps

It is situated in such a prime
location very close to the raging
fire and in direct line of the TV

THOUGHTS

There is one person who likes the
bar stool

He feels so comfortable sat on the
stool

The first thing he does is order
his drink and has his newspaper
delivered

He sups at his pint and begins
the crossword

He is deep in thought whilst he
contemplates many of the
crossword clues

Sat on his favourite stool

THE YEARS

*The years have flown past and it
does not seem like five minutes
since we started messaging one
another*

But how far have we progressed

*I know we haven't got very far
at all*

*Because we are online who knows
who you are and what is your
true story*

*I am an adult and I know what
this is all about*

Does it hurt anyone, who knows

THOUGHTS

It could go on for many more years

Who knows

AYE UP

The door opens and in steps
husband and wife

She says "Aye Up" how is
everyone?

The lady speaks with a very
strong Yorkshire accent

The lady from "Ull" someone
shouts don't you mean hull

Yes, that's what I said "Ull"

People laugh, not at her but more
so because of her strong accent

THOUGHTS

It is something southerners are not used to

And it is good to have yet another Northerner in the village

BORING

Life was so humdrum I was
plodding along and then you
came along and changed
everything

Suddenly you made my life come
alive

Instead of black and white and
the awful greys of life

I was hit with an explosion of
colour and excitement

It was just like fireworks
exploding in the dark night sky

THOUGHTS

My stomach performed summersaults

My passion for you has never ebbed

I continue to see so much colour in my life

OH YES

He does so like to be heard, in a good way

As he stands at the corner of the bar

As soon as there is an interesting conversation wafting around the bar area his antenna soon picks up on key words

Suddenly, he thrusts a hand onto his hip and he assume the position and is in full flight

"no no, listen, I think it was like this"

THOUGHTS

His booming voice resounds all around the bar area and he is off

Ten to the dozen

He does talk a lot of sense, he is very much like an actor preparing for their part in a play

The hand on the hip is only removed when he finished what he has said

He ends most conversations by saying "No I am only saying; do you know what I mean"

A LONG AWAITED ARRIVAL

It has taken so long for spring to
arrive this year

But no matter how late its
arrival

As soon as the sun bathes the
land and it soon brings its
warmth, it can be forgiven for its
lateness

The weather can be inspirational
in so many ways

The bees and butterflies are soon
out foraging the birds are
chirping away

THOUGHTS

The sights and sounds of nature
soon abound

For once nature can be forgiven
for its lateness

LUCY

He arrives with such a big grin
on his face with his cheeks so rosy
looking

He has an accomplice with him

Lucy has been for a walk with
her master?

He stands with a grin on his face,
as he stands at the bar "Oh a
class of wine please, as I have
been walking the dog"

He soon drinks the glass of wine

THOUGHTS

*"I must shoot off as the dog is
getting restless, I should be
walking her you know"?*

And with that he leaves the pub

*As he leaves he is still grinning
with by now very rosy cheeks*

FROM THE DARKNESS

Winters are hard on the psyche
and one's mind

It is as though nature is forcing
me into a tiny box within four
walls

It is dark both inside and outside

It is such a relief to be rid of the
darkness as the spring arrives

It is though a dark hood has been
lifted from my eyes

I thrive in the light not in
darkness

HUMDRUM

Life was so humdrum and boring
just plodding along and suddenly
you came from out of the blue

Life soon changed for the better

You helped make my world come
alive

It felt like fireworks going off in
the dark night sky

For the first time in a very long
time I could see what was in
front of me

You helped to turn my life upside
down

ONE DAY

One day my luck will eventually
change for the better

One day someone will help
change my life for the better

One day I may share my life with
another

One day

Who knows what will happen

One day I will not be looking
anymore

One day I will know, it will be
you

VIRTUAL

I See you virtually each day

You "pop" up and will chat to me
nothing has changed

But change it has

What right do you have coming
into my life?

Did you not think, you could just
come into my life and not have
some sort of an affect, on me?

How very wrong you are

RUNNING FREE

As I approach the field in mid winter and with snow covering the ground

Four deer could be seen running across a field suddenly all four come to an immediate stop all as one, they listened just as my boots crunch on the freshly laid snow

In the distance I could see the deer standing still and spotted me approaching

I take up my camera to try and take pictures of the deer but alas they moved on

THOUGHTS

Just as the snow begins to fall, the deer have vanished in the snow

Within seconds, it was both animal and man observing each other from a distance

It felt like back to basics

It was mother nature sharing the beauty of the wild

It was as though man had been trespassing into the deer's natural environment

STILLNES

Outside in the coldness of winter
the sounds in the stillness of the
cold air travels a long way

The cold air allows the tiniest of
sounds to travel on a carpet of
stillness abounding within the
forest

The winter makes a normal walk
in the forest, feel so magical

It feels as though it is like a
totally different world a world
not many people ever get to
experience

A little like Narnia

A CONNECTION

Who knows whatever happens
between two people when a
connection is made between
strangers

Could it be chemical reaction
deep within the brain or is it
something the eyes can see?

It is said the eyes are the
gateway to a person's soul

Or is it just the connection
between a person's eyes and
when the eyes send a message to
the brain to begin a chemical
reaction

THOUGHTS

To spark a connection

RELAX

Sundays can be very peculiar
days

It is a day to have a long lay in
bed and to read the papers

But for others it is a time to be
extremely busy and to perhaps
do the jobs which have been put
off in the garden

Or is it to have a lunchtime to
walk to a village pub and to
enjoy a roast and a pint

And for everything to be
crammed in before Monday
morning arrives

THE ONE

Within a group of people there is
always the one person who will
catch the eye

One who will always stand out
from the crowd

Someone who has a fixed smile
and pretty eyes

So young and looking pretty

SOMEONE

*Oh, how I wait for the day
someone can make my heart race
and to take my breath away*

*Someone with whom I don't have
to impress the connection is
immediate*

*Someone I can be myself with
and someone who will
understand me*

*Someone I can understand and
not have to pry open Pandora's
box*

*Someone to enjoy their company
and to enjoy life*

VIEWS

*Standing looking across the fields
from a copse*

*The scene laid out before my eyes
is very peaceful and surreal*

*It seems so surreal because we
live in a world seen from a
screen be it a computer or TV*

*There isn't a sound breaking the
stillness*

*Nothing can compare with the
scene before me*

Not even a picture on a screen

THOUGHTS

*Nature needs to be seen through
the eye and not through a lens*

ATTENTION

Oh, how she is the centre of
attention

She stands across from me
messing about with her hair

She chats to everyone who are
gathered around her

She looks very happy and is so
pretty

Life is so short, and it is there to
be grabbed with both hands and
to enjoy what we have

RIDDLES

My dear friend, if I can call you
a friend

For so many years you have
talked to me in riddles, and we
always end up going around in
circles

Time has finally run out for us

It has been with much sorrow it
has ended this way

All because of your riddle speak

TOGETHER

One day I know we will be
together and the thought keeps
me going

Knowing I will be one day with
you

I hope you feel the same way as I
do

To be able to touch your soft skin
will send my senses into
overdrive

Together is all that matters

LIFE

Life isn't as easy or as straight
forward as one wants

If it was so easy life would be
boring and very mundane

We all wish for life to be easy and
straight forward it is most
people's wish

It is difficult on ones own but
with a couple they have their
own thoughts and views

Compromise makes life tick along

CLOCK

*If I could wind back the clock
maybe if I could have had the
opportunity*

*But then the life I have now
would never have existed*

*Would I have been as rich with
the knowledge I have now?*

ANOTHER

My true feelings are for another,
we have been in contact for such
a long time

Even now I don't know what you
want from me

You have never been clear with
your true feelings for me

But despite all of this you are
always on my mind

On lonely days you jump into my
thoughts

No matter what we are going
through

Made in the USA
Columbia, SC
22 June 2018